Simply
Sweet
Crochet

Simply Sweet Crochet

Boutique Designs for Little Girls

Cony Larsen

Design Originals

an Imprint of Fox Chapel Publishing
www.d-originals.com

ISBN 978-1-57421-375-1

© 2014 by Cony Larsen and New Design Originals Corporation, www.d-originals.com, an imprint of Fox Chapel Publishing, 800-457-9112, 1970 Broad Street, East Petersburg, PA 17520.

Cony Larsen Patterns © 2014 CAD Design LLC.
Madison, Lucy, and Amelia McMurray and Veronica Moya photographs used with permission.

Special thanks to Lisa Dexheimer of Uncommon Threads, York, PA (www.uncommonthreads-pa.com) for supplying yarn for photography.

Printed in China
First printing

ACQUISITION EDITOR
Peg Couch

COPY EDITOR
Colleen Dorsey

COVER AND LAYOUT DESIGNER
Lindsay Hess

EDITOR
Katie Weeber

TECHNICAL EDITOR
Charles Voth

Introduction

"I want to feel proud to be a crocheter," one of my students said; she also expressed her concerns about the absence of new and updated crochet patterns on the market today. *Simply Sweet Crochet* is my response to these concerns!

Simply Sweet Crochet starts with basic designs for novices. Then, you can move on to mastering techniques such as those used for the Reversible Vintage Headband (page 20) and the layering technique used for the Double Delight Hat (page 34).

Don't be intimidated! All of these projects and techniques are great for beginners and will allow you to build your skills. Discover creative and fun designs with projects like the Ponytail Hat (page 42), and the just dreamy Big Cozy Cowl Hat (page 30).

I hope my collection of one-of-a-kind designs will not only inspire you to pick up your hooks and crochet, but that they will also help create a new generation of crocheters! Go ahead, be proud to be a crocheter!

Cony Larsen

Crochet Terms and Measurements

US measurements and crochet terms are used throughout the instructions in this book. For UK measurements and crochet terms, please refer to the conversion charts on pages 63 and 64.

Contents

Pom-Pom Necklace

Skill level: Beginner

 Finished size:
One size fits all

 Hook size:
G/6 (4.25mm)

 Materials:
Cascade Heritage Sock Yarn, superwash, colors of choice. This is a great project to use up any leftover yarn you may have in your stash. Use any yarn that yields 6–7 sts/in.

 Gauge:
Gauge is not essential for this project.

 Additional supplies:
None

Simply Sweet Suggestion

Attach pom-poms to a purchased headband for a quick, adorable project!

POM-POMS

Make 3 pom-poms, size 1½". You can make each one a different color, or use your yarn remnants to make multicolor ones. Leave a 6" tail on each pom-pom to attach to cording.

CORDING

With three different color skeins of yarn tog, leave a 12" tail before you start to ch.

Ch 47, twist ch so back of chain is facing you.

Row 1: Sl st in 2nd ch from hook, work through the back bar of chains only, sl st in each ch across. Fasten off, leaving a 12" tail. Make a knot with all three strands at the base of the tail, make a 2nd knot midway, and make a 3rd knot at the end of all strands. Trim off excess. Tie 3 knots evenly spaced at opposite end. Trim excess.

FINISHING

Attach pom-poms to cording about ½" apart.

Bows for Headbands

Skill level: Beginner

  Finished size:
Bow is 4¼" long by 2½" wide

 Hook size:
B/1 (2.25mm), F/5 (3.75mm)

 Materials:
Cascade Heritage Sock Yarn, superwash,
#5630 Anis (1 ball, 100g/437yd)

 Gauge:
Gauge is not essential for this project.

 **Additional supplies:**
Purchased headband of choice, hot glue gun

LARGE BOW

Make a Magic Ring (see page 61).

Row 1: Ch 1, 3 sc in Magic Ring, ch 1, turn (3 sts).

Row 2: 2 sc in first sc, sc in next sc, 2 sc in last sc, ch 1, turn (5 sts).

Row 3: 2 sc in first sc, sc in next 3 sc, 2 sc in last sc, ch 1, turn (7 sts).

Rows 4–7: Continue to increase 2 sc in first sc and 2 sc in last sc of each row, ch 1, turn (15 sts).

Rows 8–23: Sc in first sc and in each sc across, ch 1, turn.

Row 24: Sc2tog in first 2 sc, sc in next 11 sc, sc2tog in next 2 sc, ch 1, turn (13 sts).

Row 25: Sc2tog in first 2 sc, sc in next 9 sc, sc2tog in next 2 sc, ch 1, turn (11 sts).

Rows 26–28: Continue to decrease in first and last 2 sc of each row, ch 1, turn (5 sts).

Row 29: Sc in each sc across, ch 1, turn (5 sts).

Row 30: 2 sc in first sc, sc in next 3 sc, 2 sc in last sc, ch 1, turn (7 sts).

Rows 31–34: Continue to increase 2 sc in first sc and 2 sc in last sc of each row, ch 1, turn (15 sts).

Rows 35–50: Sc in first sc and in each sc across, ch 1, turn.

Rows 51–55: Rep Rows 24 through 28, ch 1, turn (5 sts).

Row 56: Sc2tog in first 2 sc, sc in next sc, sc2tog in next 2 sc, ch 1, turn (3 sts). Join ends tog with sl st. Fasten off. Weave in ends.

SMALL BOW

I made a small bow to be stacked on top of the large bow before attaching it to the headband. You can also make this small bow, or continue to the Bow Strap instructions on page 10.

Make a Magic Ring (see page 61).

Row 1: Ch 1, 3 sc in Magic Ring, ch 1, turn (3 sts).

Row 2: 2 sc in first sc, sc in next sc, 2 sc in last sc, ch 1, turn (5 sts).

Row 3: 2 sc in first sc, sc in next 3 sc, 2 sc in last sc, ch 1, turn (7 sts).

Rows 4–6: Continue to increase 2 sc in first sc and 2 sc in last sc of each row, ch 1, turn (13 sts).

Rows 7–23: Sc in first sc and in each sc across, ch 1, turn (13 sts).

Row 24: Sc2tog in first 2 sc, sc in next 9 sc, sc2tog in next 2 sc, ch 1, turn (11 sts).

Row 25: Sc2tog in first 2 sc, sc in next 7 sc, sc2tog in next 2 sc, ch 1, turn (9 sts).

Rows 26–28: Continue to decrease 2 sc in first 2 sc and dec 2 sc in last sc of each row, ch 1, turn (5 sts).

Bows for Headbands *(continued)*

Row 29: Sc in each sc across, ch 1, turn (5 sts).

Row 30: 2 sc in first sc, sc in next 3 sc, 2 sc in last sc, ch 1, turn (7 sts).

Rows 31–33: Continue to increase 2 sc in first sc and 2 sc in last sc of each row, ch 1, turn (13 sts).

Rows 34–50: Sc in first sc and in each sc across, ch 1, turn (13 sts).

Rows 51–55: Rep Rows 24 through 28, ch 1, turn (5 sts).

Row 56: Sc2tog in first 2 sc, sc in next sc, sc2tog in next 2 sc, ch 1, turn (3 sts). Join ends tog with sl st. Fasten off. Weave in ends.

BOW STRAP

Ch 5.

Row 1: Sc in 2nd ch from hook and in each ch across, ch 1, turn (4 sts).

Row 2–13: Sc in each sc across, ch 1, turn. Fasten off, leaving an 8" tail to sew after you wrap strap around bows.

CORD HEADBAND (OPTIONAL)

You can attach your bow to a purchased headband, or make a cord headband like the one in the photo above following these instructions. Measure and cut 14 yards of yarn; fold in half twice. With hook F/5 (3.75mm), crochet a chain using all strands. Fasten off. Trim ends.

ASSEMBLY

Fold bow in half with narrow ends to the center. Stack small bow on top of large bow. Wrap bow strap around both bows and join ends together with sl st. block (see page 59). Hot glue bows to a purchased headband, or make the cord headband above! Bows can also be used to embellish hats, purses, shoes, and dress collars.

Flower Headband

Skill level: Beginner

Finished size:
Flower is 3" in diameter; straps for headband are 26" long. One size fits all.

Hook size:
F/5 (3.75mm)

Materials:
Cascade 220 Superwash, #884 Skyline Blue (1 ball, 100g/220yd)

Gauge:
5 sts = 1" / 4½ rows = 1". Gauge is not essential for this project.

Additional supplies:
Safety pins, tapestry needle

FLOWER

Make a Magic Ring (see page 61).

Rnd 1: Ch 2, [(3 dc, ch 2, sl st) in ring** ch 2] 5 times ending final rep at ** (5 petals).

Rnd 2: [Ch 3, sl st between next 2 petals] 5 times (5 ch-3 sps).

Rnd 3: Ch 1, [(sl st, ch 2, 5 dc, ch 2, sl st) in next ch-3 sp] 5 times (5 petals).

Rnd 4: [Ch 4, sl st between next 2 petals] 5 times (5 ch-4 sps).

Rnd 5: Ch 1, [(sl st, ch 2, 4 dc, ch 3, 4 dc, ch 2, sl st) in next ch-4 sp] 5 times (5 petals).

Fasten off.

CORDING

Ch 110, fasten off, leaving a 10" tail.

With back of flower facing up and 10" tail in tapestry needle, weave one end of first cord through upper half of back of petals from Rnd 5. Parallel to first end, weave other end of first cord through lower half of back of petals from Rnd 5. Sew ends of cord to each other, being careful not to twist cord. Slide woven cord through back of flower so sewn ends are behind center of flower and two long loops are on opposite sides of flower. Fold these loops and mark the center chain on each loop with a safety pin.

Ch 40, sl st to marked st on folded loop of first cord, ch 22, sl st to back of Rnd 4 between parallel strands of first cord, ch 6, sl st to back of Rnd 4 opposite first sl st, ch 22, sl st to marked st on second folded loop of first cord, ch 40, fasten off.

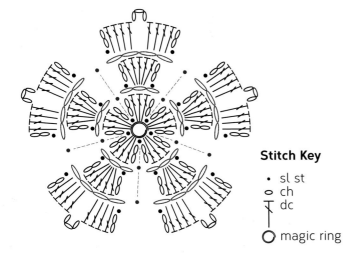

Stitch Key

- •   sl st
- o   ch
- ⊤   dc
- O   magic ring

Spring Headband

Skill level: Beginner

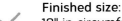

✓ **Finished size:**
18" in circumference, 1½" wide. Flowers are 2" in diameter.

✎ **Hook size:**
D/3 (3.25mm)

🧶 **Materials:**
Sublime Baby Cashmere Merino Silk DK yarn (1 ball, 50g/20yd per flower). If desired, use leftover yarn from your stash.

✥ **Gauge:**
Gauge is not essential for this project.

+ **Additional supplies:**
Tapestry needle, pins, small buttons

HEADBAND (OPTIONAL)

Ch 9.

Row 1: Ch 1, sl st in 2nd ch from hook, sl st in every ch across, ch 1, turn.

Row 2: Sl st in back loop only of sl st across, ch 1, turn.

Rows 3-104: Rep Row 2 until headband measures 18" or until desired length is achieved. Join ends tog with sl st. Fasten off. Weave in ends.

Simply Sweet Suggestion

Make a headband for this project following the instructions above, or attach the flowers and leaves to a purchased headband as shown in the photo below.

FLOWERS

Make 5 flowers in the colors you desire as follows:

Ch 6, join with sl st to first ch to form a ring.

Rnd 1: Ch 1, *sc in ring, crochet a bobble (see below) in ring, sc in ring; rep from * around 5 times. Join with sl st in beg sc (6 bobbles). Fasten off. Weave in ends.

How to Make a Bobble

Ch 4, 5 dtr, leave the last loop of each dtr on hook (6 loops on hook). Then, yo and draw a loop through all loops on hook to complete stitch, ch 4.

Spring Headband *(continued)*

LEAVES

Ch 8.

Sc in 2nd ch from hook. Sc in next ch, hdc in next ch, dc in next 2 chs, tr in next 2 chs, ch 3, sl st in same st as last tr. Work on opposite side of chs, ch 3, tr in next 2 chs, dc in next 2 chs, hdc in next ch, sc in last 2 chs. Join with sl st to beg sc. Fasten off, leaving a 6" tail. Thread 6" tail through a tapestry needle and do a running stitch to make the center vein of leaf (see photo below).

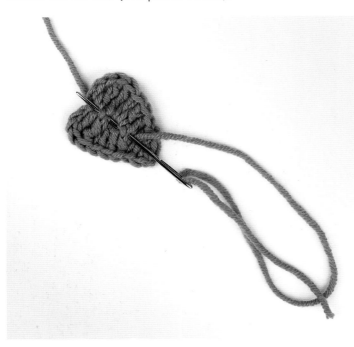

Stitch Key

- • sl st
- o ch
- + sc
- ‡ dc
- ‡ tr

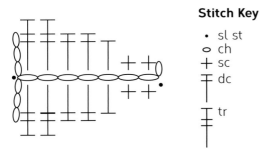

FINISHING

Place flowers on headband and secure in place with pins. With a tapestry needle, sew flowers onto headband (see photos below). Sew small buttons in the center of each flower. To make leafy grass, thread tapestry needle with a 12" yarn strand, and create leafy grass as shown in photo below. Trim off excess yarn.

Simply Sweet Suggestion

You may add petals to a flower by adding more bobbles (see page 14). Switching to a thicker yarn will also change the size of your flower. Keep your tension loose for fluffy petals. Use fleece yarn for luxurious, soft petals.

"Sugar and spice and all things that are nice, that's what little girls are made of."

—EARLY NINETEENTH CENTURY NURSERY RHYME

Hydrangea Headband

Skill level: Beginner

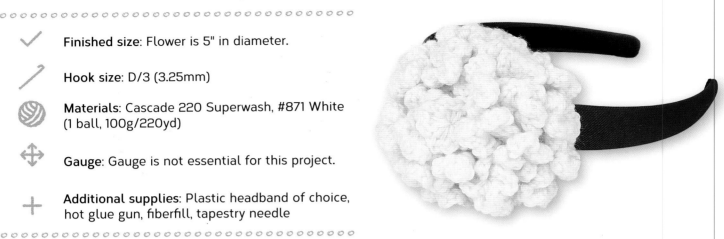

 Finished size: Flower is 5" in diameter.

 Hook size: D/3 (3.25mm)

 Materials: Cascade 220 Superwash, #871 White (1 ball, 100g/220yd)

 Gauge: Gauge is not essential for this project.

 Additional supplies: Plastic headband of choice, hot glue gun, fiberfill, tapestry needle

FLORETS

Make 35 hydrangea florets as described below. These individual florets will be attached to a circular flower base to form the finished hydrangea flower.

Make a Magic Ring (see page 61).

Rnd 1: Ch 2, make a petal as follows, [(3 dc, ch 2, sl st) in ring, ch 2] 4 times. Join with sl st to beg ch (4 petals). Fasten off, leaving a 5" tail to attach floret to flower base.

FLOWER BASE (TOP)

Make a Magic Ring (see page 61).

Rnd 1: Work 8 sc in Magic Ring. Join with sl st to beg sc (8 sts).

Rnd 2: Ch 1, 2 sc in each sc around. Join with sl st to beg sc (16 sts).

Rnd 3: Ch 1, sc in first sc, 2 sc in next sc, *sc in next sc, 2 sc in next sc; rep from * around. Join with sl st to beg st (24 sts).

Rnd 4: Ch 1, sc in first 2 sc, 2 sc in next sc, *sc in next 2 sc, 2 sc in next sc; rep from * around. Join with sl st to beg st (32 sts).

Rnds 5–7: Ch 1, sc in each sc around. Join with sl st to beg st (32 sts). Fasten off, leaving a 6" tail to join top and bottom circle flower bases.

FLOWER BASE (BOTTOM)

Make a Magic Ring (see page 61).

Rnds 1–4: Rep Rnds 1–4 of flower base top.

Rnd 5: Ch 1, sc in each sc around. Fasten off.

ASSEMBLY

Thread the 5" tail from a floret onto a tapestry needle, or use a crochet hook to pull tail through, and attach it securely to the top of the flower base. Repeat with each floret, spacing them around the flower base (see photo below). Join top and bottom circles of flower base with sl st, leaving a 1" opening; fill firmly with fiberfill, close opening with sl st. Fasten off. Weave in ends. Hot glue completed hydrangea flower to headband.

Stitch Key

- • sl st
- ○ ch
- ┬ dc
- ⭘ magic ring

Reversible Vintage Headband

Skill level: Beginner

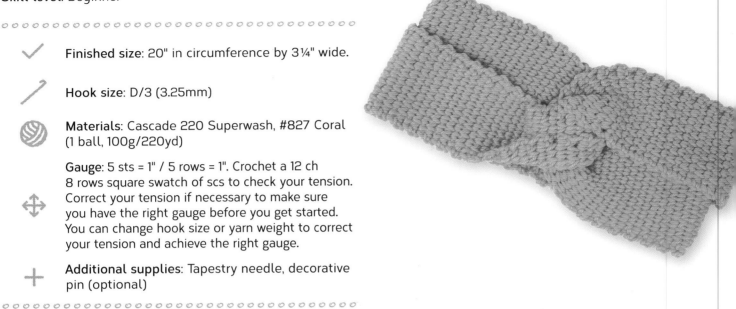

✓ **Finished size:** 20" in circumference by 3¼" wide.

╱ **Hook size:** D/3 (3.25mm)

🧶 **Materials:** Cascade 220 Superwash, #827 Coral (1 ball, 100g/220yd)

Gauge: 5 sts = 1" / 5 rows = 1". Crochet a 12 ch 8 rows square swatch of scs to check your tension. Correct your tension if necessary to make sure you have the right gauge before you get started. You can change hook size or yarn weight to correct your tension and achieve the right gauge.

╋ **Additional supplies:** Tapestry needle, decorative pin (optional)

REVERSIBLE TEXTURE

The first and last sc of each row is worked through both loops of sc. All the scs after the first sc is done are worked through the center of core of each sc from the prior row. This will create the reversible texture rather than creating a wrong and a right side as usual.

LEFT SIDE (MAIN)

Center of core

Ch 11.

Row 1: Sc in 2nd ch from hook and in each remaining ch, ch 1, turn (10 scs).

Rows 2–60: Sc through center of core of each sc across (see photo at right), sc in last sc, ch 1, turn. Work 59 more rows, or until strap measures approximately 10". Do not fasten off. Continue with instructions for left side back below.

LEFT SIDE (BACK)

Fold the strap in half lengthwise. Place the end of the strap attached to your yarn skein over the beg first row, overlapping the ends by 5 sts.

Row 1: Sc in center of core (see photo above) of first 5 sc, work 1 sc through all thicknesses of next 9 scs, sc in last sc, ch 1, turn (15 scs).

Row 2: Sc in center of core of next 14 scs, sc in last sc, ch 1, turn.

Rows 3–30: Rep Row 2 until back section measures 5". If you want a bigger headband, continue to work more rows until you achieve the desired length.

RIGHT SIDE (MAIN)

Ch 11.

Row 1: Sc in 2nd ch from hook and in each remaining ch, ch 1, turn (10 scs).

Rows 2–60: Sc in center of core (see photo at left) of each sc across, sc in last sc, ch 1, turn. Work 59 more rows, or until strap measures approximately 10". Do not fasten off.

Take right side main section and interlock with left side main section as seen in photo above; continue with instructions for right side back below.

RIGHT SIDE (BACK)

Fold strap in half lengthwise. Place the end of the strap attached to your yarn skein over the beg first row, overlapping ends by 5 sts.

Row 1: Sc in center of core (see photo at left) of first 5 sc, work 1 sc through all thicknesses of next 9 scs, sc in last sc, ch 1, turn (15 scs).

Row 2: Rep instructions for left side back section.

Rows 3–30: Rep instructions for left side back section.

FINISHING

Join the ends of the left side and right side sections together with sl st. Fasten off. Weave in ends. With a tapestry needle, sew folds in place. Leave as is or attach a decorative pin on the folds.

Reversible Heart Headband

Skill level: Beginner

Finished size: 12½" long by 6½" wide. After attaching the hearts, the length is 15". Braided ties are 15" long.

Hook size: F/5 (3.75mm)

Materials: Cascade 220 Superwash, #871 White and #884 Skyline Blue or other contrasting color of your choice for hearts (1 ball each color, 100g/220yd)

Gauge: 4½ sts = 1" / 6 rows = 1". Crochet a 12 ch 8 rows square swatch of scs to check your tension. Correct your tension if necessary to make sure you have the right gauge before you get started. You can change hook size or yarn weight to correct your tension and achieve the right gauge.

Additional supplies: Tapestry needle, safety pins

REVERSIBLE TEXTURE

The first and last sc of each row is worked through both loops of sc. All the scs after the first sc is done are worked through the center of core of each sc from the prior row. This will create the reversible texture, rather than creating a wrong and a right side as usual.

RIGHT SIDE

Ch 14.

Row 1: Sc in 2nd ch from hook and in each remaining ch, turn (13 sc).

Row 2: Ch 1, sc in next 6 sc (see Reversible Texture note above), [sc between posts of sc below and next sc], sc in next sc, rep between [ ] (increase just made, see photo at right), sc in next 6 sc, turn (15 sc).

Row 3: Ch 1, sc in each sc across, turn.

Row 4: Ch 1, sc in next 7 sc, [sc between posts of sc below and next sc], sc in next sc, rep between [ ], sc in next 7 sc, ch 1, turn (17 sc).

Row 5: Rep Row 3.

Row 6: Ch 1, sc in next 8 sc, [sc between posts of sc below and next sc], sc in next sc, rep between [ ], sc in next 8 sc, ch 1, turn (19 sc).

Row 7: Rep Row 3.

Row 8: Ch 1, sc in next 9 sc, [sc between posts of sc below and next sc], sc in next sc, rep between [ ], sc in next 9 sc, ch 1, turn (21 sc).

Row 9: Rep Row 3. You may stop at this row to make a headband that is not as wide.

Row 10: Ch 1, sc in next 10 sc, [sc between posts of sc below and next sc], sc in next sc, rep between [ ], sc in next 10 sc, ch 1, turn (23 sc).

Row 11: Rep Row 3.

Row 12: Ch 1, sc in next 11 sc, [sc between posts of sc below and next sc], sc in next sc, rep between [ ], sc in next 11 sc, ch 1, turn (25 sc).

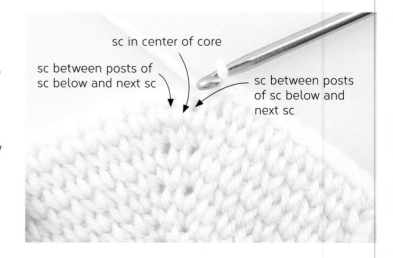

sc in center of core

sc between posts of sc below and next sc

sc between posts of sc below and next sc

Reversible Heart Headband *(continued)*

Row 13: Rep Row 3.

Row 14: Ch 1, sc in next 12 sc, [sc between posts of sc below and next sc], sc in next sc, rep between [ ], sc in next 12 sc, ch 1, turn (27 sc).

Row 15: Rep Row 3.

Row 16: Ch 1, sc in next 13 sc, [sc between posts of sc below and next sc], sc in next sc, rep between [ ], sc in next 13 sc, ch 1, turn (29 sc).

CENTER

Continue to follow previous instructions for reversible texture.

Rows 1–32: Sc through both loops of first sc, sc in center of core of each sc from prior row in next 27 sc, sc through both loops of last sc (29 sc).

Note: You may add more rows to increase size at this point, or work fewer rows to decrease size and achieve the desired size.

LEFT SIDE

Continue to follow previous instructions for reversible texture.

Row 1: Ch 1, sc through both loops of first sc, sc in next 12 sc, sk next sc, sc in next sc, sk next sc, sc in next 12 sc, sc through both loops of last sc, turn (27 sc).

Row 2: Ch 1, sc in each sc across, turn.

Row 3: Ch 1, sc through both loops of first sc, sc in next 11 sc, sk next sc, sc in next sc, sk next sc, sc in next 11 sc, sc through both loops of last sc, turn (25 sc).

Row 4: Rep Row 2, turn.

Row 5: Ch 1, sc through both loops of first sc, sc in next 10 sc, sk next sc, sc in next sc, sk next sc, sc in next 10 sc, sc through both loops of last sc, turn (23 sc).

Row 6: Rep Row 2, turn.

Row 7: Ch 1, sc through both loops of first sc, sc in next 9 sc, sk next sc, sc in next sc, sk next sc, sc in next 9 sc, sc through both loops of last sc, turn (21 sc).

Row 8: Rep Row 2, turn.

Row 9: Ch 1, sc through both loops of first sc, sc in next 8 sc, sk next sc, sc in next sc, sk next sc, sc in next 8 sc, sc through both loops of last sc, turn (19 sc).

Row 10: Rep Row 2, turn.

Row 11: Ch 1, sc through both loops of first sc, sc in next 7 sc, sk next sc, sc in next sc, sk next sc, sc in next 7 sc, sc through both loops of last sc, turn (17 sc).

Row 12: Rep Row 2, turn.

Row 13: Ch 1, sc through both loops of first sc, sc in next 6 sc, sk next sc, sc in next sc, sk next sc, sc in next 6 sc, sc through both loops of last sc, turn (15 sc).

Row 14: Rep Row 2, turn.

Row 15: Ch 1, sc through both loops of first sc, sc in next 5 sc, sk next sc, sc in next sc, sk next sc, sc in next 5 sc, sc through both loops of last sc, turn (13 sc).

Row 16: Rep Row 2, turn. Do not fasten off; you will continue to work the edging.

EDGING

Rnd 1: Ch 1, working on long side of headband at the end of each row, *sk first row, sl st in next row; rep from * to end of side. 2 sc in last row for corner, sc across narrow end of headband, 2 sc in last sc for corner, **ch 1, sk next row, sl st in next row; rep from ** to end of side. 2 sc in last row for corner, sc across narrow end of headband. Join with sl st to first ch. Fasten off. Weave in ends.

BRAIDED TIES

Cut 1 strand of yarn about 20yd long. Fold yarn strand in half 5 times until it measures about 22" long. Find the center of the 22" bundle and tie a string around it to hold the strands in place while you braid (see photo below). Clip the ends to make 32 individual strands. Divide the strands into three groups, two groups of 11 strands each, and one group of 10 strands. Braid the three groups together, leaving the last 2" unbraided to create a tassel. Cut a string 10" long and tie it at end of braid, just above 2" left free for tassel. Trim ends. Repeat to make a second braided tie.

HEARTS

Size: 4" wide by 3" high

Make 2 hearts.

Ch 12.

Rnd 1: 2 sc in 2nd ch from hook, sc in next 3 chs, **ddec** (see Special Stitches below), sc in next 3 chs, 4 sc in last ch; work on other side of chs, sc in next 4 chs, 3 sc in next ch, sc in next 4 chs, 2 sc in last ch. Join with sl st to beg sc (26 sc).

Rnd 2: Ch 1, 2 sc in each of next 2 sc, sc in next 2 sc, ddec, sc in next 2 sc, 2 sc in each of next 4 sc, sc in next 5 sc, 3 sc in next sc, sc in next 5 sc, 2 sc in last 2 sc. Join with sl st to beg sc (34 sc).

Rnd 3: Ch 1, 2 sc in each of next 2 sc, sc in next 3 sc, ddec, sc in next 3 sc, 2 sc in each of next 4 sc, sc in next 8 sc, 3 sc in next sc, sc in next 8 sc, 2 sc each of last 2 sc. Join with sl st to beg sc (42 sc).

Rnd 4: Ch 1, 2 sc in each of next 2 sc, sc in next 4 sc, sl st in next sc, sk next sc, sl st in next sc, sc in next 4 sc, 2 sc in each of next 4 sc, sc in next 11 sc, 3 sc in next sc, sc in next 11 sc, 2 sc in each of last 2 sc. Join with sl st to beg sc. Fasten off, weave in ends (51 sc).

Rnd 5: Ch 1, sl st in first sc, *ch 1, sl st in next sc; rep from * around. Join with sl st to beg st. Fasten off, weave in ends (102 sts).

{ ### Special Stitches
Double decrease (ddec): [insert hook in next st, yo, draw up a loop], sk next ch or st, rep between [ ], yo, draw through all loops on hook. }

FINISHING

With a tapestry needle, attach the braided ties to each end of headband. Place hearts over each end of headband and braided ties and hold in place with safety pins. Using the tapestry needle and matching yarn, stitch hearts to each end of headband as shown below. To make the headband reversible, make 2 more hearts in a different color for 4 hearts total. After you have secured the braided ties to the headband, place headband ends and braided ties between two different colored hearts, back to back. Hold hearts in place with safety pins, and stitch hearts together.

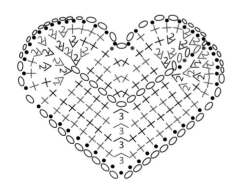

Stitch Key

- • sl st
- ○ ch
- + sc
- ✕✕ ddec
- ⅄ 2 sc in same st
- 3 sc in same st

Pom-Pom Headband

Skill level: Beginner

 Finished size: 21" in circumference by 4" wide, size fits 10-year-old to young adult. For different sizes, change the number of chainless foundation single crochet stitches worked in round one.

 Hook size: F/5 (3.75mm)

 Materials: Cascade 220 Superwash, #900 Charcoal (1 ball, 100g/220yd)

 Gauge: 5 sts = 1" / 4½ rows = 1". Crochet a 12 ch 8 rows square swatch of scs to check your tension. Correct your tension if necessary to make sure you have the right gauge before you get started. You can change hook size or yarn weight to correct your tension and achieve the right gauge.

+ Additional supplies: Tapestry needle, pom-pom maker

TOP SECTION

This project is worked in rows (back and forth) and joined with a sl st to the beg of each row.

Rnd 1: Work 84 cfsc (see page 60).

Rnd 2: Ch 1, sc in first sc, *dc in next sc, sc in next sc, rep from * around. Join with sl st to beg sc, ch 1, turn.

Rnd 3: Sc in first dc, *dc in next sc, sc in next dc, rep from * around. Join with sl st to beg sc, ch 1, turn.

Rnds 4-12: Rep Rnd 2 until headband measures approx. 3¼" from beg or to desired width.

EDGING

Rnd 1: Ch 1, sl st in first st, *dc in next sc, sl st in next dc; rep from * around. Join with sl st to beg sc. Fasten off. Weave in ends.

Attach yarn to opposite edge of headband, ch 1, sl st in first sc, *dc in next sc, sl st in next dc; rep from * around. Join with sl st to beg sc. Fasten off. Weave in ends.

FRONT STRAP

Ch 9.

Rnd 1: Sc in 2nd ch from hook, *dc in next st, sc in next dc; rep from * across, ch 1, turn (8 sts).

Rnd 2: Sc in first dc, *dc in next sc, sc in next dc; rep from * across, ch 1, turn.

Rnd 3: Rep Rnd 2, do not fasten off.

ATTACHING THE FRONT STRAP

The front strap is used to hold the pleats of the headband in place. You can then add a pom-pom over the front strap if desired, or leave the pom-pom off. Find your headband's seam (a "seam" is created at the end of each row where you join each round) and pleat it. Take your front strap and wrap it around pleated part; sl st ends of strap tog. Fasten off, leaving a 10" tail. Thread 10" tail through a tapestry needle and secure strap to headband with a few stitches.

POM-POM

If desired, make a 4" pom-pom and secure to front of headband. I recommend using the large or extra-large Pom-Pom Maker by Clover to make your pom-pom. I wrapped the yarn around only one-half of the pom-pom maker, following manufacturer's instructions.

Simply Sweet Suggestion

I'm always looking for ways to spice up my crochet projects. I love the variety of embellishments available, from buttons to ribbons to silk flowers. Your local craft or scrapbook store is a great place for ideas. Next time you crochet a headband or hat, try adding some decorations—the choices are endless.

Pom-Pom Cowl

Skill level: Beginner

 Finished size: 32" in diameter by 4½" wide, size fits 10-year-old to adult.

 Hook size: F/5 (3.75mm)

 Materials: Cascade 220 Superwash, #900 Charcoal (1 ball, 100g/220yd)

 Gauge: 5 sts = 1" / 4½ rows = 1". Crochet a 12 ch 8 rows square swatch of scs to check your tension. Correct your tension if necessary to make sure you have the right gauge before you get started. You can change hook size or yarn weight to correct your tension and achieve the right gauge.

 Additional supplies: Pom-pom maker

TOP SECTION

This project is worked in rows (back and forth) and joined with a sl st to the beg of each row.

Rnd 1: Work 90 cfsc (see page 60). Join with sl st to beg sc, being careful not to twist ch.

Rnd 2: Ch 1, sc in first sc, *dc in next sc, sc in next sc, rep from * around. Join with sl st to beg sc, ch 1, turn.

Rnd 3: Sc in first dc, *dc in next sc, sc in next dc, rep from * around. Join with sl st to beg sc, ch 1, turn.

Rnds 4–5: Rep Rnd 2 until cowl measures approx. 1¾" from beg.

Rnd 6: Sc in first sc, *ch 1, sk next st, sc in next st; rep from * around. Join with sl st to beg sc, ch 1, turn.

Rnd 7: *Sc in ch sp, dc in next sc; rep from * around. Join with sl st to beg sc, ch 1, turn.

Rnd 8-11: Rep Rnd 2 until cowl measures approx. 3½" from beg, do not ch and turn after Rnd 11.

Rnd 12: Ch 1, *sc in next st, ch 1, sc in next st; rep from * around. Join with sl st to beg sc (180 sts).

Rnd 13: Ch 1, *sc in ch sp, dc in next sc; rep from * around. Join with sl st to beg sc (180 sts).

EDGING

Rnd 1: Ch 1, sl st in first st, *dc in next st, sl st in next st; rep from * around. Join with sl st to beg st (180 sts). Fasten off. Weave in ends.

BOTTOM SECTION

Flip work and join with sl st to beg st on the opposite side of the foundation row.

Rnd 1: Ch 1, sc in first sc, *dc in center of core of next sc, sc in center post of next sc; rep from * around. Join with sl st to beg sc, ch 1, turn.

Rnd 2: Sc in first sc, *dc in next sc, sc in next sc; rep from * around. Join with sl st to beg sc, ch 1, turn.

Rnd 3: *Sc in next st, ch 1, sc in next st; rep from * around. Join with sl st to beg sc (180 sts).

Rnd 4: Ch 1, *sc in ch sp, dc in next sc; rep from * around. Join with sl st to beg sc (180 sts).

Rnd 5: Rep Rnd 1 of edging.

CORDING

Make a 28" cord as follows:

Leave a 1" tail and then ch 140.

Rnd 1: Sl st in 2nd ch from hook and in each ch across. Fasten off, leaving a 10" tail. You will use 10" tail to attach decorative pom-poms.

Weave cording through the ch spaces from Round 6 of the top section. Attach a pom-pom to each end.

POM-POMS

If desired, make a 2" and a 3" pom-pom and secure to ends of cording. I recommend using the small or large Pom-Pom Maker by Clover to make your pom-poms.

Big Cozy Cowl Hat

Skill level: Beginner

Finished size: Cowl is 27" in circumference around shoulders. Hood is 9" deep, size fits 3- to 5-year-old.

Hook size: G/6 (4.25mm)

Materials: Cascade 220 Superwash, #818 Mocha (2 balls, 100g/220yd each)

Gauge: 4 sts = 1" / 4½ rows = 1". Crochet a 12 ch 8 rows square swatch of scs to check your tension. Correct your tension if necessary to make sure you have the right gauge before you get started. You can change hook size or yarn weight to correct your tension and achieve the right gauge.

Additional supplies: Stitch marker, tapestry needle, two 1¼" wood buttons

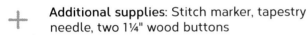

Special Stitches
Shell (sh): Work (sc, ch 1, dc) in indicated stitch.

HOOD

Row 1: Work 46 cfsc (see page 60).

Row 2: (RS) Ch 1, sc in first 2 sts, *sh (see Special Stitches at top of right column) in next st, sk 2 sts; rep from * across to last 2 sts, sc in each of last 2 sts, ch 1, turn (46 sts, 14 sh).

Rows 3–73: Rep Row 2 until rectangle measures approx. 19" or desired length. Do not fasten off. Place st marker on 7th st from beg of Row 73.

Fold rectangle in half lengthwise, with wrong sides tog. Working through both layers, join back seam tog with sl sts. Fasten off, weave in ends.

COWL

Rnd 1: Beginning marked st, sl st to join, ch 1, sc in same st, sc in next 79 st, ch 11, leave remaining sts unworked. Join with sl st to beg sc, ch 1, turn (91 sts).

Rnd 2: Sc in first 3 sts, *ch 1, sc in next 2 sts; rep from * around. Join with sl st to beg sc, ch 1, turn (135 sts).

Rnd 3: Sh in same st as join, *sk 2 sts, sh in next st; rep from * around, ending with sk 2 sts. Join with sl st to beg sc, ch 1, turn (135 sts, 45 shs).

Rnds 4–12: Rep Rnd 3.

RIBBED EDGING

Rnd 1: Sc in first sc, ch 1, sk next st or ch, *sc in next st or ch, ch 1, sk next st or ch; rep from * around. Join with sl st to beg sc, do not turn (134 sts).

Rnds 2–6: Ch 1, sc in same st as sl st from previous rnd, ch 1, *sc in front loop only of next sc, ch 1; rep from * around. Join with sl st to first st, do not turn.

Fasten off. Weave in ends.

FINISHING

Fold edge of hood back about 1½" to form a cuff. Attach wood buttons to each side of hat with tapestry needle to hold cuff back.

Peter Pan Collar

Skill level: Beginner

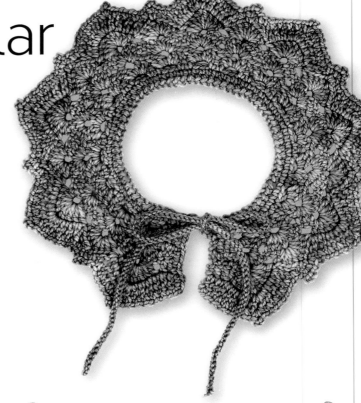

 Finished size: Collar is 11¾" in diameter. Size fits 3-year-old or younger.

 Hook size: 4 (1.75mm)

 Materials: Cascade Heritage Sock Yarn, superwash, #5603 Marine (1 ball, 100g/437yd)

 Gauge: 7–8 sts = 1" / 5 rows = 1". Gauge is not essential for this project.

+ **Additional supplies:** None

COLLAR

Work 70 cfsc (see page 60).

Row 1: Ch 1, turn, sc in first sc and in each sc across (70 sts).

Row 2: Ch 1, sc in first 2 sc, *ch 3, sk next 2 sc, sc in next 2 sc*; rep from * to * around. Join with sl st to beg sc (17 ch-3 sps).

Row 3: Ch 2, dc in first 2 sc, **sh1** (see Special Stitches at right) in first ch-3 sp, *sk next 2 sc, sh1 in next ch-3 sp; rep from * across, dc in last 2 sc.

Row 4: Ch 2, dc in first 2 dc, **sh2** (see Special Stitches at right) in each ch-2 sp across, dc in last 2 sc.

Row 5: Ch 2, dc in first 2 dc, **sh3** (see Special Stitches at right) in each ch-2 sp across, dc in last 2 sc.

Row 6: Ch 2, dc in first 2 dc, *[dc in next dc, ch 1] 4 times, (dc, ch 1, dc, ch 1) in ch-2 sp, [dc in next dc**, ch 1] 4 times, ch 1, sk next 4 dc, sc in next ch-2 sp, ch 2*; rep from * across, ending final rep at **, dc in last 2 sc.

Row 7: Ch 1, sc in first 2 dc, *[ch 1, sk next dc, sc in ch-1 sp] 4 times, ch 1, **picot** (see Special Stitches at right) in ch-2 sp, [ch 1, sk next dc, sc in ch-1 sp] 4 times**, ch 1, sc in ch-2 sp, ch 1, picot in next sc, ch 1, sc in ch-2 sp; rep from * across, ending final rep at **, ch 1, sc in last 2 sc. Do not fasten off.

FINISHING

Edging: Rotate work 90 degrees. Work 9 sc evenly across edge sts of Rows 7–1. (Sc, ch 3, sc) in corner st, (sc, ch 1) in each st across opposite side of foundation sts. (Sc, ch 3, sl st) in corner st. Join with sl st to beg sc. Fasten off. Weave in ends.

Cording: Ch 110, sl st in each ch across. Fasten off. Weave in ends. Thread cord through front loops at each corner of collar.

Special Stitches

Shell 1 (sh1): Work (2dc, ch 2, 2dc) in ch-3 sp.
Shell 2 (sh2): Work (3dc, ch 2, 3dc) in ch-2 sp.
Shell 3 (sh3): Work (4dc, ch 2, 4dc) in ch-2 sp.
Picot: Work (sc, ch 1, sc) in indicated sp/st.

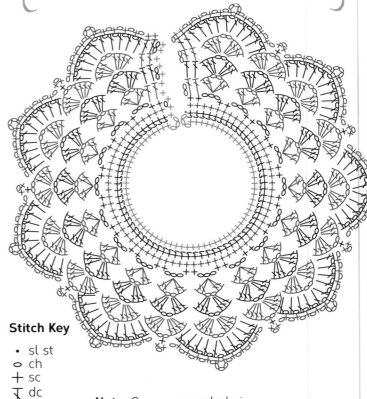

Stitch Key

- • sl st
- o ch
- + sc
- ┬ dc
- ⌇ cfsc

Note: Green sc symbols in diagram represent edging sc.

Double Delight Hat

Skill level: Beginner

✓ **Finished size:** Ages 0-6 mos (7-12 mos, 2 yrs, 3-6 yrs), circumference 13½" (16", 17¼", 18¾")

✎ **Hook size:** B/1 (2.25mm)

🧶 **Materials:** Sublime Baby Cashmere Merino Silk 4 Ply yarn, #51 Button and #123 Sleepy or other contrasting color of your choice (1 ball each color, 50g/184yd)

✥ **Gauge:** 6 sts = 1" / 6 rows = 1". Crochet a 12 ch 8 rows square swatch of scs to check your tension. Correct your tension if necessary to make sure you have the right gauge before you get started. You can change hook size or yarn weight to correct your tension and achieve the right gauge.

➕ **Additional supplies:** None

Note: Instructions for child size hat in parentheses.

CROWN

This beautiful pattern is very simple. You will need to work scs alternating one in the front loop and one in the back loop throughout the entire pattern.

Ch 32; join with sl st to beg ch to form a ring, being careful not to twist chain.

Rnd 1: Ch 1, sc in same st, ch 1, *sk next ch, sc in next ch, ch 1; rep from * around. Join with sl st to beg sc (32 sts [16 sc and 16 ch]).

Rnd 2: Ch 1, sc in front loop of first sc, *sc in back loop of ch, sc in front loop of next sc*; rep from * around. Join with sl st to beg sc (32 sts).

Rnd 3: Ch 1, 2 sc in same st as sl st join, *[sc flo in next sc, sc blo in next sc] 7 times**, 3 sc in next sc; rep from * around, ending final rep at **, sc in next sc. Join with sl st to beg sc (40 sts).

Rnd 4: Ch 1, 2 sc in same st as sl st join, *[sc blo in next sc, sc flo in next sc] 9 times**, 3 sc in next sc; rep from * around, ending final rep at **, sc in next sc. Join with sl st to beg sc (48 sts).

Rnd 5: Ch 1, 2 sc in same st as sl st join, *[sc flo in next sc, sc blo in next sc] 11 times**, 3 sc in next sc; rep from * around, ending final rep at **, sc in next sc. Join with sl st to beg sc (56 sts).

Rnds 6-8: Alternating, rep Rnds 4 and 5, continue to work scs, alternating 1 in flo and 1 in blo, and then increasing 3 sc at each corner (80 [96, 104, 112] sts).

BODY

Rnds 1-3 (3, 4, 5): Ch 1, working in established flo/blo pattern, work sc in each st around. Join with sl st to beg sc.

Rnd 4 (4, 5, 6): Ch 1, sc blo of each sc around (the front loop will be used later to start the upper lace). Join with sl st to beg sc.

Rnds 5-22 (18, 20, 20): Ch 1, working in established flo/blo pattern, work sc in each st around. Join with sl st to beg sc.

Rnd 23 (23, 26, 27): Ch 1, sc blo of each sc around (the front loop will be used later to start the lower lace). Join with sl st to beg sc.

EDGING

Rnd 1: Ch 1, *sc in center post of next sc, ch 1, sk next sc; rep from * around. Join with sl st to beg sc.

Rnds 2-6: Rep Rnd 1. Fasten off.

Double Delight Hat *(continued)*

FINISHING

Lower Lace (optional): Attach contrasting color onto first front loop of first sc from Rnd 23 (23, 26, 27) from body of hat.

Rnd 1: Ch 1, sc in first st, *ch, sk next st, sc in front loop of next sc; rep from * around. Join with sl st to beg sc (10 [12, 13, 14] shells).

Rnd 2: Ch 1, sk next 3 sts, *(3 dc, ch 1, 3 dc) in next ch-1 sp, ch 1, sk (sc, ch 1, sc), sl st in next ch-1 sp, ch 1, sk (sc, ch 1, sc); rep from * around. Join with sl st to beg sc. Fasten off.

Upper Lace (optional): Attach contrasting color onto first front loop of first sc from Rnd 4 (4, 5, 6) from body of hat,

Rnds 1-2: Rep Rnds 1 and 2 of lower lace above.

Rnd 3: Sl st in next 3 dc, (sl st, ch 3, 3 dc, ch 1, 4 dc) in next ch-1 sp, (4 dc, ch 1, 4 dc) in ch-1 sp in next shell; rep from * around. Sl st to top of first ch-3 to join.

Rnd 4: Sl st in next 4 dc, (sl st, ch 3, 3 dc, ch 1, 4 dc) in next ch-1 sp, (4 dc, ch 1, 4 dc) in ch-1 sp in next shell; rep from * around. Sl st to top of first ch-3 to join.

Fasten off. Weave in ends.

Simply Sweet Suggestion

Choosing the right fiber colors for your project can be difficult. Using monochromatic colors are a safe way to go when you are a novice. Invest in a color wheel and learn how to use it to mix and match colors in a complementary way.

"Like star dust glistening on fairies' wings, little girls' dreams are of magical things."

—SHERRY LARSON

Sami's Vintage Hat

Skill level: Beginner

 Finished size: Ages 0–6 mos (7–12 mos, 2 yrs, 3–6 yrs), circumference 13" (14", 16", 20")

 Hook size: C/2 (2.75mm)

 Materials: Sublime Baby Cashmere Merino Silk 4 Ply yarn, #1 Piglet (1 ball, 50g/184yd) (2 balls for child size)

 Gauge: 25 sts = 4" / 11 rows = 4" in shell stitch pattern. Correct your tension if necessary to make sure you have the right gauge before you get started. You can change hook size or yarn weight to correct your tension and achieve the right gauge.

 Additional supplies: Tapestry needle, decorative pin (optional)

Note: Instructions for child size hat in parentheses.

CROWN

Make a Magic Ring (see page 61).

Rnd 1: Work 8 hdc in Magic Ring. Join with sl st to beg hdc (8 sts).

Rnd 2: Ch 1, 2 hdc in each st around. Join with sl st to beg st (16 sts).

Rnd 3: Ch 1, *hdc in next st, 2 hdc in next st; rep from * around. Join with sl st to beg st (24 sts).

Rnd 4: Ch 1, *hdc in next 2 sts, 2 hdc in next st; rep from * around. Join with sl st to beg st (32 sts).

Rnd 5: Ch 1, *hdc in next 3 sts, 2 hdc in next st; rep from * around. Join with sl st to beg st (40 sts).

Rnd 6: Ch 1, *hdc in next 4 sts, 2 hdc in next st; rep from * around. Join with sl st to beg st (48 sts).

Rnd 7: Ch 1, *hdc in next 5 sts, 2 hdc in next st; rep from * around. Join with sl st to beg st (56 sts).

Ages 0–6 mos and 7–12 mos only: Fasten off.

Ages 2 yrs and 3–6 yrs:
Rnd 8: Ch 1, *hdc in next 3 sts, 2 hdc in next st; rep from * around. Join with sl st to beg st (70 sts).

Age 2 yrs: Fasten off.

Ages 3–6 yrs:
Rnd 9: Ch 1, *hdc in next 4 sts, 2 hdc in next st; rep from * around. Join with sl st to beg st (84 sts). Fasten off.

Special Stitches
Shell (sh): Work (sc, ch 1, dc) in indicated st.

BODY

Ch 79 (88, 100, 127) sts, join with sl st to beg ch, being careful not to twist ch.

Rnd 1: Ch 1, **sh** (see Special Stitches above) in first ch, sk 2, *sh in next ch, sk 2; rep from * around, ending with sc in last st. Sl st to first sc to join, turn, 26 (29, 33, 42) sh.

Rnd 2: Ch 1, sh in first sc, *sh in next sc; rep from * around, ending with sc in last sc, sl st to first sc to join, turn.

Rep Rnd 2 until piece measures 4¼" (5", 5¼", 6¼").

FINISHING

With RS tog, join crown and body pieces tog, easing in any fullness as follows:

Sl st through first sts of both layers, sl st through next st of each layer, *sk 1 st of body, sl st through next 2 sts of each layer; rep from * around. Fasten off, leaving a 10" tail to stitch front drape. Gather at the seam for front drape; make 3 pleats to form the front center drape; sew folds in place with a tapestry needle and 10" tail. Leave drape as is or attach decorative pin.

Sami's Vintage Hat *(continued)*

BOW (OPTIONAL)

Size: 2⅛" long by 2¼" wide

Ch 3.

Row 1: Sc in 2nd ch from hook, sc in next ch, ch 1, turn (2 sts).

Row 2: 2 sc in first sc, sc between sc, 2 sc in next sc, ch 1, turn (5 sts).

Rows 3–10: Sc in each st across, ch 1, turn (5 sts).

Row 11: Sc dec in first 2 sts, sc in next st, sc dec in last 2 sts, ch 1, turn (3 sts).

Row 12: Sc dec in first 2 sts, sc in last st, ch 1, turn (2 sts).

Row 13: 2 sc in first sc, sc in next st, ch 1, turn (3 sts).

Row 14: 2 sc in first st, sc in next st, 2 sc in last st, ch 1, turn (5 sts).

Rows 15–22: Sc in each st across, ch 1, turn (5 sts).

Row 23: Sc dec in first 2 sts, sc in next st, sc dec in last 2 sts, ch 1, turn (3 sts).

Row 24: Sc dec in first 2 sts, sc in last st, ch 1, turn (2 sts).

Row 25: Sc in next 2 sts. Sew ends tog. Fasten off. Weave in ends.

BOW CENTER STRAP

Ch 16, sc in 2nd ch from hook, sc in each ch across, 2 sc in last ch, turn and crochet on the opposite side of starting ch, sc in each ch across, sc in last ch, join with sl st to beg sc. Fasten off, leaving a 10" tail to sew strap to bow and to secure bow to hat.

Simply Sweet Suggestion

You will see that the hats in this book are made of a crown, a body, and edging. You can mix and match these different sections to suit your skill level or taste. Combine the different designs to create your very own hat!

"Her smile beams like sunshine, which fills our hearts with love."

—UNKNOWN

Ponytail Hat

Skill level: Beginner

 Finished size: 19" in circumference, 7½" deep

 Hook size: G/6 (4.25mm)

 Materials: Cascade 220 Superwash, #871 White and two additional colors of your choice (1 ball each color, 100g/220yd)

 Gauge: 4 sts = 1" / 4½ rows = 1". Crochet a 12 ch 8 rows square swatch of scs to check your tension. Correct your tension if necessary to make sure you have the right gauge before you get started. You can change hook size or yarn weight to correct your tension and achieve the right gauge.

 Additional supplies: 2" elastic hair tie

CROWN

Ch 48; join with sl st to beg ch to form a ring, being careful not to twist ch.

Rnd 1: Ch 1, sc in first st, *ch, sk next st, sc in next st; rep from * around. Join with sl st to beg sc (48 sts).

Rnd 2: Ch 2 (counts as first sc), sk first sc, *sc in ch-1 space, ch 1, sk next sc; rep from * around. Join with sl st to beg ch (48 sts).

Rnds 3–4: Rep Rnds 1 and 2, alternating. Join with sl st to beg ch (48 sts).

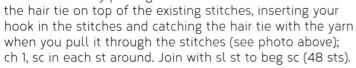

Rnd 5: In this round you are going to crochet around the elastic hair tie by placing the hair tie on top of the existing stitches, inserting your hook in the stitches and catching the hair tie with the yarn when you pull it through the stitches (see photo above); ch 1, sc in each st around. Join with sl st to beg sc (48 sts).

Rnd 6: Ch 1, sc in first sc and in each sc around. Join with sl st to beg sc.

Rnd 7: Ch 1, *sc in next 5 sc, 2 sc in next sc; rep from * around. Join with sl st to beg sc (56 sts).

Rnd 8: Ch 1, sc in each sc around. Join with sl st to beg sc.

Rnd 9: Ch 1, *sc in next 6 sc, 2 sc in next sc; rep from * around. Join with sl st to beg sc (64 sts).

Rnd 10: Ch 1, sc in each sc around. Join with sl st to beg sc.

Rnd 11: Ch 1, *sc in next 7 sc, 2 sc in next sc; rep from * around. Join with sl st to beg sc (72 sts).

Rnd 12: Ch 1, *sc in each sc around. Join with sl st to beg sc.

Rnd 13: Ch 1, *sc in next 5 sc, 2 sc in next sc*, rep from * to * around. Join with sl st to beg sc, (84 sts).

Rnd 14: Ch 1, *sc in each sc around. Join with sl st to beg sc.

Rnd 15: Ch 1, *sc in next 6 sc, 2 sc in next sc*, rep from * to * around. Join with sl st to beg sc, (96 sts).

You may add another round to make hat bigger. Each round increases the size of the hat by 2" or 8 sts.

BODY

Rnds 1–12: Ch 1, sc in first sc, *ch 1, sk 1, sc in front loop only of next sc*; rep from * to * around. Join with sl st to beg sc.

Rnds 13–16: Change to contrasting color, ch 1, rep Rnd 1. Join with sl st to beg sc.

Rnds 17–20: Change to white, ch 1, rep Rnd 1. Join with sl st to beg sc.

Continue until hat measures 7½" from start, or to desired depth. Fasten off.

EDGING

Rnd 1: With second contrasting color, join with sl st to bottom edge of hat, ch 2 (counts as first sc), *sc in ch-1 space, sk next sc, ch 1; rep from * around. Join with sl st to beg ch.

Rnd 2: Ch 1, dc in first ch-1 space, *sl st in next sc, dc in ch-1 space; rep from * around. Join with sl st to beg dc. Fasten off. Weave in ends.

Coco's Soft Alpaca Newborn Hat

Skill level: Beginner

 Finished size: 16" in diameter by 6" from crown to bottom edge

 Hook size: C/2 (2.75mm), B/1 (2.25mm)

 Materials: Blue Sky Alpacas Royal Petites yarn, #1713 Laurel (1 ball, 35g/100yd) (2 balls for a larger infant size hat)

 Gauge: 6–7 sts = 1" / 7 rows = 1". Crochet a 12 ch 8 rows square swatch of scs to check your tension. Correct your tension if necessary to make sure you have the right gauge before you get started. You can change hook size or yarn weight to correct your tension and achieve the right gauge.

 Additional supplies: None

CROWN

Make a Magic Ring (see page 61).

Rnd 1: 12 sc in Magic Ring. Join with sl st to beg sc (12 sts).

Rnd 2: Ch 1, sc in each sc. Join with sl st to beg sc.

Rnd 3: Ch 1, 2 sc in each st around. Join with sl st to beg st (24 sts).

Rnd 4: Rep Rnd 2.

Rnd 5: Ch 1, *sc in next st, 2 sc in next st; rep from * around. Join with sl st to beg st (36 sts).

Rnd 6: Rep Rnd 2.

Rnd 7: Ch 1, *sc in next 2 sts, 2 sc in next st; rep from * around. Join with sl st to beg st (48 sts).

Rnd 8: Rep Rnd 2.

Rnd 9: Ch 1, *sc in next 3 sts, 2 sc in next st; rep from * around. Join with sl st to beg st (60 sts).

Rnd 10: Rep Rnd 2.

Rnd 11: Ch 1, *sc in next 4 sts, 2 sc in next st; rep from * around. Join with sl st to beg st (72 sts).

Rnd 12: Rep Rnd 2.

Rnd 13: Ch 1, *sc in next 5 sts, 2 sc in next st; rep from * around. Join with sl st to beg st (84 sts).

Rnd 14: Rep Rnd 2.

Rnd 15: Ch 1, *sc in next 6 sts, 2 sc in next st; rep from * around. Join with sl st to beg st (96 sts).

Rnd 16: Rep Rnd 2.

Rnd 17: Ch 1, *sc in next 7 sts, 2 sc in next st; rep from * around. Join with sl st to beg st, (108 sts, 5¾").

BODY

Rnd 1: Ch 1, sc in front loop only of first sc, *ch 1, sk next st, sc in front loop only of next sc; rep from * around, end with sc in last 2 sc. Join with sl st to front loop only of beg sc.

Rnd 2–20: Rep Rnd 1 until body measures approx. 5" from crown.

RIBBED BAND

With hook B/1 (2.25mm), work all scs through the center of core of each sc rather than through the top loops of each sc.

Rnd 1: Ch 1, sc through center of core of first sc, *ch, sk next st, sc through center of core of next sc*; rep from * to * around. Join with sl st to beg sc (108 sts).

Rnds 2–5: Ch 1, rep Rnd 1. Join with sl st to beg sc. If you are not planning on doing the edging, you may fasten off at this point. Weave in ends.

CROCHET EDGING (OPTIONAL)

Rnd 1: Ch 2, sl st in next st, *ch, sl st in next st; rep from * around. Join with sl st to beg st. Fasten off. Weave in ends.

Woven Flowers Hat

Skill level: Beginner

Finished size: Ages 0–6 mos (7–12 mos, 2 yrs, 3–6 yrs), circumference 13¾" (15½", 17", 19")

Hook size: C/2 (2.75mm)

Materials: Sublime Baby Cashmere Merino Silk 4 Ply yarn, #4 Gooseberry (1 ball, 50g/184yd), 5yd each of pink, lavender, and yellow yarn of your choice. This is a great project for using up any leftover yarn you may have in your stash. Use any yarn that yields 6–7 sts/in.

Gauge: 7 sts = 1" / 6 rows = 1". Crochet a 12 ch 8 rows square swatch of scs to check your tension. Correct your tension if necessary to make sure you have the right gauge before you get started. You can change hook size or yarn weight to correct your tension and achieve the right gauge.

Additional supplies: None

Note: Instructions for child size hat in parentheses.

CROWN

Make a Magic Ring (see page 61).

Rnd 1: 12 sc in Magic Ring. Join with sl st to beg sc (12 sts).

Rnd 2: Ch 1, sc in each sc. Join with sl st to beg sc (12 sts).

Rnd 3: Ch 1, sc in first sc, *ch 2, sc in next sc; rep from * around. Join with sl st to beg st (12 sc, 12 ch-2 sps).

Rnd 4: Ch 1, sc in first sc, *ch 2, sk 2 chs, sc in next sc; rep from * around. Join with sl st to beg sc (12 sc, 12 ch-2 sps).

Rnd 5: Ch 1, 2 sc in first sc, *ch 2, sk 2 chs, 2 sc in next sc; rep from * around. Join with sl st to beg sc (24 sc, 12 ch-2 sps).

Rnd 6: Ch 1, sc in first sc, 2 sc in next sc, *ch 2, sk 2 chs, sc in next sc, 2 sc in next sc; rep from * around (36 sc, 12 ch-2 sps).

Rnd 7: Ch 1, sc in first 2 sc, 2 sc in next sc, *ch 2, sk 2 chs, sc in next 2 sc, 2 sc in next sc; rep from * around (48 sc, 12 ch-2 sps).

Rnd 8: Ch 1, sc in first 3 sc, 2 sc in next sc, *ch 2, sk 2 chs, sc in next 3 sc, 2 sc in next sc; rep from * around (60 sc, 12 ch-2 sps).

Rnd 9: Ch 1, sc in first 4 sc, 2 sc in next sc, *ch 2, sk 2 chs, sc in next 4 sc, 2 sc in next sc; rep from * around (72 sc, 12 ch-2 sps).

Rnd 10: Ch 1, sc in first 5 sc, 2 sc in next sc, *ch 2, sk 2 chs, sc in next 5 sc, 2 sc in next sc; rep from * around (84 sc, 12 ch-2 sps).

For 3 larger sizes, continue in same manner, increasing 12 sc evenly around every rnd until you have (96, 108, 120) sc and 12 ch-sps.

BODY

Rnd 1: Ch 2, hdc in first 7 (8, 9, 10) sc, *ch, hdc in next 7 (8, 9, 10) sc; rep from * around (84 [96, 108, 120] hdc, 12 ch-1 sps).

Rnds 2–17: Rep Rnd 1 until body measures approx. 4" (5", 5¾", 6¼") from beg or to desired length.

EDGING

Rnd 1: Ch 1, sc in first sc, *ch, sk next st, sc in next st; rep from * around. Join with sl st to beg sc (96 [108, 120, 132] sts).

Rnds 2–3 (3, 4, 5): Ch 1, sc in center post of first sc, *ch, sk next ch, sc in center post of next sc; rep from * around. Join with sl st to beg sc.

CORDS

Make 12 cords, 4 of each pink, lavender, and yellow.

Ch 90 (94, 98, 102). Fasten off, leaving a 10" tail to attach cord to flower.

Woven Flowers Hat (continued)

FLOWERS

Make 12 flowers, 4 of each pink, lavender, and yellow.

Make a Magic Ring (see page 61).

Rnd 1: [(sc, hdc, dc, hdc, sc) in Magic Ring] 5 times. Join with sl st to beg sc. Fasten off. Weave in ends through center of flower; pull short tail of Magic Ring tight to close center of flower.

FINISHING

Weave in cords through the ch sps on the hat, begin at one edge of hat, and end at opposite edge of hat; attach a flower at end of each cord.

Stitch Key

- • sl st
- + sc
- ⊤ hdc
- ⊤ dc
- ◯ magic ring

Simply Sweet Suggestion

Wondering how to adjust the pattern for a different size? Hat sizes can be adjusted by using larger hook sizes or greater yarn weight or by adding more pattern repetitions/stiches. See the sizing notes in the hat projects for more details.

"A daughter is one of
the most beautiful gifts
this world has to give."

—LAUREL ATHERTON

Coral Hearts Hat

Skill level: Beginner

 Finished size: 18½" (20") in diameter by 7" (7¾") from crown to bottom edge. Size fits 1- to 2-year-old (3- to 5-year-old).

 Hook size: F/5 (3.75mm)

 Materials: Cascade 220 Superwash, #818 Mocha for hat, #817 Coral for hearts (1 ball each color, 100g/220yd)

 Gauge: 5 sts = 1" / 5 rows = 1". Crochet a 12 ch 8 rows square swatch of scs to check your tension. Correct your tension if necessary to make sure you have the right gauge before you get started. You can change hook size or yarn weight to correct your tension and achieve the right gauge.

+ Additional supplies: Tapestry needle

Note: Instructions for 3- to 5-year-old hat in parentheses.

CROWN

Make a Magic Ring (see page 61)

Rnd 1: 12 sc in Magic Ring. Join with sl st to beg sc (12 sts).

Rnd 2: Ch 1, sc in each sc. Join with sl st to beg sc (12 sts).

Rnd 3: Ch 1, 2 sc in each sc. Join with sl st to beg st (24 sts).

Rnd 4: Rep Rnd 2 (24 sts).

Rnd 5: Ch 1, *sc in next sc, 2 sc in next st; rep from * around. Join with sl st to beg sc (36 sts).

Rnd 6: Rep Rnd 2 (36 sts).

Rnd 7: Ch 1, *sc in next 2 sts, 2 sc in next st; rep from * around. Join with sl st to beg sc (48 sts).

Rnd 8: Rep Rnd 2 (48 sts).

Rnd 9: Ch 1, *sc in next 3 sts, 2 sc in next st; rep from * around. Join with sl st to beg sc (60 sts).

Rnd 10: Rep Rnd 2 (60 sts).

Rnd 11: Rep Rnd 9 (75 sts).

Ages 1–2 yrs only: Ch 1, 2 sc in first sc, *sc in next 5 sts, ch 1; rep from * around, end with sc in last 4 sc, ch 1. Join with sl st to beg sc (91 sts, 5" in diameter).

Ages 3–5 yrs only: Ch 1, *sc in next 3 sts, ch 1; rep from * around, end with ch 1. Join with sl st to beg sc (100 sts, 5" in diameter).

BODY

Worked in joined rows.

Rnd 1: (RS) Ch 1, sh in first sc (see Special Stitches above), *sk 2 sts, sh in next st; rep from * around, end with sc in last st (30 [33] sh). Join with sl st to beg sc, ch 1, turn (91 [100] sts).

Rnd 2: Sh in first sc, *sk 2 sts, sh in next sc; rep from * around, end with sc in last st (30 [33] sh). Join with sl st to beg sc, ch 1, turn (91 [100] sts).

Rnds 3–14: Rep Rnd 2 until body measures approx. 3½" (4") from beg, or to desired depth, ending with a WS round.

BAND

Rnd 1: Sc in first st, *ch 1, sk next st, sc in next st; rep from * around, end with sc in last st. Join with sl st to beg sc (91 [100] sts).

Rnds 2–6: Ch 1, sc in center post of first sc, *ch 1, sk next ch, sc in center post of next sc; rep from * around, end with sc in last st. Join with sl st to beg sc (91 [100] sts).

Coral Hearts Hat *(continued)*

CORD TIES

Ch 60, sl st in 2nd ch from hook, sl st in each ch across. Fasten off, leaving a 10" tail to attach to hat.

Use hat as is or make two hearts (see below) for earflaps.

HEARTS

Make 2 hearts following the instructions on page 25.

FINISHING

If possible, try the hat on your child to mark the placement of the heart earflaps. Otherwise, mark center of each side of hat for ears; then mark 1" towards back of head. Center hearts on latter marks with valley of heart at the lower edge of the band. With a tapestry needle, stitch hearts to hat with running stitch. Secure cord ties to hearts with yarn.

"Little girls are precious gifts,
wrapped in love serene.
Their dresses tied with sashes
and futures tied with dreams."

—UNKNOWN

Harvest Hat

Skill level: Beginner

 ✓ **Finished size:** Ages 0–6 mos (7–12 mos, 2 yrs, 3–6 yrs), circumference 14" (15", 17", 19")

 Hook size: F/5 (3.75mm), G/6 (4.25mm)

 Materials: Sublime Baby Cashmere Merino Silk DK yarn, #285 Orange (1 ball, 50g/184yd), 4yd contrasting color yarn for edging, 24" elastic beading cord, 100% wool yarn for felted pansy (optional)

 Gauge: 6 sts and 6 rows = 1"

 Additional supplies: Tapestry needle, stitch marker, pins, brad or button

Special Stitches

Spike St (spst): Insert hook in corresponding st 1 row below next st, yo, pull up loop to height of current row, yo, pull through 2 loops on hook.

Note: Instructions for child size hat in parentheses.

CROWN

Ch 4; join with sl st to beg ch to form a ring.

Rnd 1: Ch 1, 9 sc in ring. Join with sl st to beg sc.

Rnd 2: Ch 1, 2 sc in each sc around. Join with sl st to beg sc (18 sts).

Rnd 3: Ch 1, *sc in next 2 sc, 2 sc in back loop only of next sc; rep from * around, end with 2 sc in last sc. Join with sl st to beg sc (24 sts).

Rnd 4: Ch 1, *sc in next 3 sc, 2 sc in back loop only of next sc; rep from * around, end with 2 sc in last sc. Join with sl st to beg sc (30 sts).

Rnd 5: Ch 1, *sc in next 4 sc, 2 sc in back loop only of next sc; rep from * around, end with 2 sc in last sc. Join with sl st to beg sc (36 sts).

Continue in this manner, increasing at the points of the hexagon shape that has formed until there are 84 (90, 102, 114) sts around.

BODY

Mark beg of round with stitch marker.

Rnds 1–15: Ch 1, *sc in next 13 (14, 16, 18) sts, sc in back loop only of next st; rep from * around. Join with sl st to beg sc.

Cut a piece of elastic beading cord 1" longer than the chosen circumference size. Tie ends together without trimming the excess.

Rnd 16: Hold elastic cord on top of stitches, ch 1, sc in each sc, catching the elastic cord under each st (see photo on page 42). Join with sl st to beg sc. Fasten off. Weave in ends.

EDGING

Rnd 1: Join contrasting yarn color between any two sc near beg of round 1; ch 1, *spst (see Special Stitches at left), ch 3, sk 1 sc; rep from * around. Join with sl st to beg sc. Finish off accent color. Weave in ends.

Harvest Hat *(continued)*

FELTED PANSY

You can make the pansy using purchased 100% wool felted sheets, or you can felt your own sheet as follows:

With hook size G/6 (4.25mm) and 100% wool yarn in contrasting color, crochet loosely, ch 32.

Row 1: Dc in 3rd ch from hook, dc in each ch across, turn.

Row 2: Ch 2, dc in each st across, turn. Rep row 2 until you have a rectangle that measures 6" x 13". Finish off. Felt rectangle (see page 58 for felting instructions). Cut flower layers following the instructions below.

FINISHING

Trace and cut one of each of the three flower patterns below from paper. Use pins to secure patterns to felted rectangle and cut. Stack flower layers from largest to smallest. Use a brad or a button as a center for the flower and secure to the top of the hat with a tapestry needle.

Felted Pansy Flower Layers
(pattern appears at actual size)

"Every child is a
different kind of flower,
and all together,
they make this world
a beautiful garden."

—UNKNOWN

Techniques

FELTING

Felting may be done using two different methods depending on the size of the project: hand felting or machine felting. Machine felting is very simple and great for larger projects. Hand felting is my preferred method. It wastes less water, gives you more control over the finished size, and is great for small projects. However, it is more labor intensive. Choose which method will work best for you. The best yarns for felting are 100% wool yarns. Acrylic and polyester yarns, or yarns labeled "superwash," will not felt. Make sure your project is completely finished before felting, because you won't be able to weave in ends once the project is felted.

Several elements may change the outcome of felting. Crocheted items will require more felting time than knitted items, as crochet stitches are more closely formed than knitting stitches. Also, items crocheted or knitted with small hooks or needles will have tighter stitches, which do not allow for enough friction for felting between the stitches.

Machine Felting

Supplies: Gather a mesh laundry bag or small pillowcase, 2 tennis balls, a pair of old jeans, and ¼ cup mild laundry detergent (the tennis balls and jeans help with agitation). Make sure the jeans are old and well washed so there is no risk of their color bleeding onto your project.

Set your washing machine for the smallest load (to save water), the hottest temperature (the heat opens up the layers of the fibers), cold rinse (this will close the fibers and set the felting), and the longest cycle (to allow enough time for felting). Add the detergent, which will allow the fibers to rub and slide easily. Place your project pieces and the tennis balls inside your mesh bag and close it. Put the bag in your washing machine with the jeans and start the machine.

Once the wash is complete, remove your project pieces and see if you like the results. If you can still see the

stitch definition, repeat the process. You may need to repeat the process several times until you have achieved the desired size and look.

To finish, remove the project from the mesh bag once you are satisfied with the results. Form it back into its proper shape. I like to stuff my projects with white paper napkins or paper towels until they have the desired shape. Let dry.

Hand Felting

Supplies: Gather a container, 1 golf ball (for agitation), 4–6 drops of mild liquid soap, and 2 cups of boiling water. These materials will vary based on the size of your project. Small projects can be felted using a 28 oz. plastic blender container with a screw-on lid. Larger projects will require larger containers, with more soap and water.

For small projects: Boil 2 cups of water and pour them into your container. Add the golf ball and your project. Let everything sit for 30 minutes, making sure your project is completely saturated. After the water has cooled, add the soap. Agitate everything by shaking the container vigorously for 5–10 minutes. Remove the lid and pour out the water. Squeeze the excess water from your project and check your progress. If the piece is not felted as desired, repeat the process.

For large projects: Soak your completed project in hot water in a large container with a lid for 30 minutes. Make sure the project is completely saturated. Add soap. Agitate the piece by rubbing and kneading it in the water. When the water cools, add more hot water. Be patient, as this may take some time. Check your progress and repeat the process until the piece is felted as desired.

To finish, rinse your project with cool water. Roll the item in a towel and squeeze out any excess water—do NOT wring the project or you risk pulling it out of shape. Form the project back into its proper shape. I like to stuff my projects with white paper napkins or paper towels until they have the desired shape. Let dry.

Finishing Your Project

BLOCKING

Always check the yarn label for any special care instructions. Many natural fibers, such as cotton, linen, and wool, respond well to steam blocking. However, you shouldn't use steam or heat on mohair or angora. Many acrylics and some blends shouldn't be blocked at all, especially with steam, because they can melt.

Use a hand towel or handkerchief and a padded ironing board. If you prefer, you can substitute a table or any flat surface that you have padded adequately.

Take the dampened towel or handkerchief, place it over the edge of the project, and steam with an iron, holding the iron slightly above the finished project. Lift the towel and repeat with another section all the way around. Leave the project in place until it is dry.

TIPS AND NOTES

Shopping: Buy all skeins of yarn or crochet cotton you will need to finish your project at the same time. There is no guarantee that your local retailer will have the same yarn lot and color in stock when you run out. You should also have the right hook sizes and other supplies before you get started.

Tension, tension, tension: I cannot express how important tension is in crochet. It's the difference between "handmade" and "homemade." If you crochet too tightly, your project will curl up; if you crochet too loosely, it will start to ruffle. Correct your tension as needed by holding the thread tighter or looser. You can also switch your hook size to achieve the right gauge.

Practice: Practice makes perfect (but avoid perfection!). The only way to correct your tension is to practice. Remember, though: after all is said and done, your crochet project exists ultimately to show your love for your family and friends. A simply decorated gift that features a beautiful edge is priceless. This is supposed to be fun! If you are not having fun, reevaluate.

Fibers, color, technique, and accents: There are four basic elements to a well thought-out gift: fiber quality, color matching, technique, and, as desired, accents (hardware or embellishments). Your fiber quality and color matching are the most important elements of your project. Don't give up fiber quality for cheaper substitutes. Your project will have a better finish, and it will pass the tests of frequent use and time if you use quality materials.

Texture: Even if textured fibers lure you, using them effectively can be a challenge. When using textured yarn, make sure you know how the project will look when it's finished. Read the manufacturer's care instructions. If your project is a garment that will be used often or will be used by a child, pick a fiber that will handle regular washing without falling apart.

Dos and don'ts: Keep it simple. Plan and read instructions before you get started. Go back and redo any step if you're not pleased with the tension or other results. Take a class to learn the basics. Keep your fibers protected in a yarn/thread dispenser while you work on your project. Don't wait for the perfect moment to get started.

Stitch Guide

CHAINLESS FOUNDATION SINGLE CROCHET

A Chainless Foundation Single Crochet chain allows you to work a foundation row/round that will have the same stretching properties as your last row/round. Traditionally, the first row is made with a number of chains and then you work scs across chains. This method limits the stretching ability of your first row. Unlike a traditional first row, foundation stitches will stretch the same as your last row, ideal for headbands, gloves, and afghans.

Setup: Ch 2, insert hook in 2nd ch from hook, yo, pull up a loop, ch 1, place stitch marker in first st from hook, yo, pull through 2 loops on hook (foundation st made).

Additional stitches: *Insert hook in marked ch, yo, pull up a loop, ch 1, move marker to first st from hook, yo, pull through 2 loops on hook (1 more foundation sc made); rep from * as many times as necessary to achieve indicated stitch count.

1 Ch 2.

2 Insert hook in 2nd ch from hook, yo, pull up a loop.

3 Place stitch marker in first st from hook (see arrow).

4 Yo.

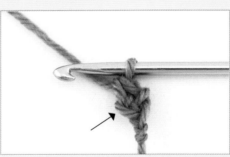

5 Pull through 2 loops on hook (foundation st made). *Insert hook in marked ch.

6 Yo, pull up a loop.

7 Ch 1, move marker to first st from hook.

8 Yo, pull through 2 loops on hook (1 more foundation sc made).

9 Rep from * (in Step 5) as many times as necessary to achieve indicated stitch count.

Stitch Guide *(continued)*

MAGIC RING

A magic ring, also know as an adjustable ring or magic circle loop, is a starting technique for crocheting in rounds by creating a loop that allows you to put the stitches in; you can then draw the loop up tight to leave no visible hole in the center.

1 Leaving a 10" tail, wind the yarn from the yarn ball around your fingers as shown.

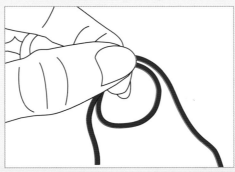

2 Grasp the yarn at the top where the strands overlap.

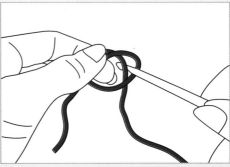

3 Insert hook through the front of the ring and grab the yarn.

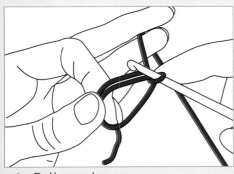

4 Pull up a loop.

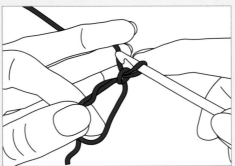

5 Chain 1; this chain is to "lock" the magic ring, it is not part of your stitch count. You may pull on the yarn to tighten the lock.

6 Chain 1, *insert hook through ring, yarn over, and pull through both loops on hook* (single crochet made) repeat from * to * to make as many single crochets as the pattern requires.

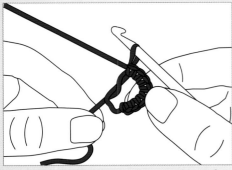

7 After completing the number of stitches in the ring, grab the tail and pull firmly to close the ring.

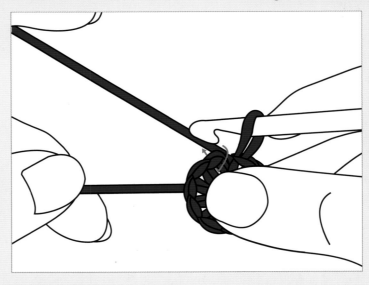

8 Join ring with slip stitch by inserting hook through both loops of beginning single crochet (see pink arrow); don't insert hook through beginning "lock" stitch. Pull the tail again tightly to close center completely.

Stitch Guide *(continued)*

Holding the hook

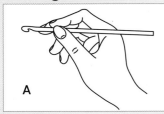

A   B

Holding the yarn

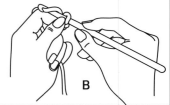

A   B

Slip knot

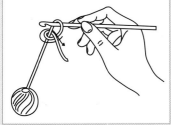

Start with a slip knot on your hook.

Yarn over (yo)

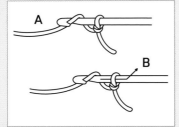

A

B

Yarn over (yo), pull through loop (lp) on hook.

Chain (ch)

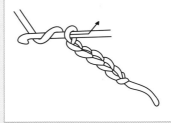

Yarn over (yo), pull through loop (lp) on hook.

Slip stitch (sl st)

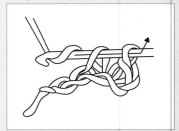

Insert hook in stitch (st), pull through both lps on hook.

Single crochet (sc)

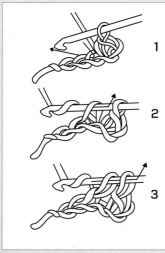

1

2

3

Insert hook in st, yo, pull through st, yo, pull through both lps on hook.

Half double crochet (hdc)

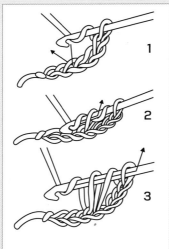

1

2

3

Yo, insert hook in st, yo, pull through st, yo, pull through all 3 lps on hook.

Double crochet (dc)

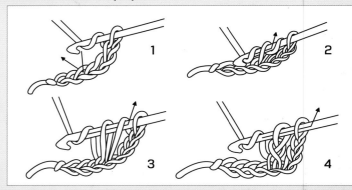

1

2

3

4

Yo, insert hook in st, yo, pull through st, [yo, pull through 2 lps] twice.

Treble crochet (tr)

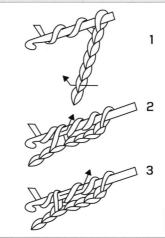

1

2

3

Yo twice, insert hook in st, yo, pull through st, [yo, pull through 2 lps] 3 times.

Double treble crochet (dtr)

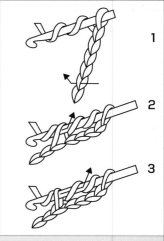

1

2

3

Yo 3 times, insert hook in st, yo, pull through st, [yo, pull through 2 lps] 4 times.

Front/back loop (front lp/back lp)

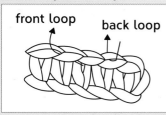

front loop   back loop

Changing colors

To change colors, drop the first color. With the second color, pull through last lp of st.

Stitch Guide *(continued)*

Single crochet two together (sc2tog) or single crochet decrease (sc dec)

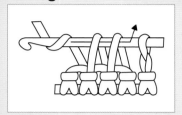

This allows you to single crochet 2 or more sts together. (Insert hook, yo, draw lp through) in each of the sts indicated, yo, draw through all lps on hook.

Half double crochet decrease (hdc dec): (Yo, insert hook, yo, draw lp through) in each of the sts indicated, yo, draw through all lps on hook.

Double crochet decrease (dc dec): (Yo, insert hook, yo, draw loop through, yo, draw through 2 lps on hook) in each of the sts indicated, yo, draw through all lps on hook.

HEAD MEASUREMENTS FOR HATS AND HEADBANDS

Note: All size charts contain approximate measurements.

Measure around the head: Measure around the largest area above the eyebrows to just above the ears, and continuing across the back of the bend of the neck and around to the front of the head. Use this measurement for the circumference of the hat.

Measure front to back: Starting just above the eyebrows, measure back over the crown to the bend where the head meets the top of the neck. Use this measurement for the depth of the hat.

Measure ear to ear: Starting at the top front of one ear, measure up and over the crown to the same position on the opposite ear. Use this measurement for the length of a headband.

Baby Size Chart

Age (in mos)	0–3	3–6	6–9	9–12
Approx. head size	14"	16"	18"	19"

Child Size Chart

Age (in yrs)	2–4	5–8	9–12
Approx. head size	19"	20"	21½"

Additional Sizes

Age	Teen	Women	Men
Approx. head size	20½"–22"	21½"–22½"	23"–24"

Crochet Terms Conversion Chart

US term	UK/AUS term
end off or finish off	fasten off
sl st (slip stitch)	ss or sl st
sc (single crochet)	dc (double crochet)
hdc (half double crochet)	htr (half treble crochet)
dc (double crochet)	tr (treble crochet)
tr (treble crochet)	dtr (double treble crochet)
dtr (double treble crochet)	trip tr or trtr (triple treble crochet)
FPdc (front post dc)	rtrf (raised front treble)
BPdc (back post dc)	rtrb (raised back treble)
yo (yarn over)	yoh (yarn over hook)

Crochet Abbreviations

beg	begin
blo	back loop only
CC	contrasting color
cfsc	chainless foundation single crochet
ch(s)	chain(s)
ch sp(s)	chain space(s)
cl(s)	cluster(s)
cm	centimeters
dc	double crochet
dc dec	double crochet decrease
dec	decrease
dtr	double treble crochet
flo	front loop only
hdc	half double crochet
hdc dec	half double crochet decrease
inc	increase
lp(s)	loop(s)
MC	main color
mm	millimeters
rep(s)	repeat(s)
rnd(s)	round(s)
RS	right side
sc	single crochet
sc dec	single crochet decrease
sc2tog	single crochet two together
sk	skip
sl st(s)	slip stitch(es)
st(s)	stitch(es)
tog	together
tr	treble crochet
WS	wrong side
yd	yard
yo	yarn over

Stitch Guide (continued)

Metric Conversion Chart

US	Metric	US	Metric
¼"	0.5cm	13½"	34cm
½"	1.5cm	13¾"	35cm
1"	2.5cm	14"	35.5cm
1¼"	3cm	15"	38cm
1½"	4cm	15½"	39.5cm
1¾"	4.5cm	16"	41cm
2"	5cm	17"	43cm
2⅛"	5.5cm	17¼"	44cm
2¼"	5.5cm	18"	45.5cm
2½"	6.5cm	18½"	47cm
3"	7.5cm	18¾"	47.5cm
3¼"	8.5cm	19"	48.5cm
3½"	9cm	20"	51cm
4"	10cm	20½"	52cm
4¼"	11cm	21"	53.5cm
4½"	11.5cm	21½"	54.5cm
5"	12.5cm	22"	56cm
5¼"	13.5cm	22½"	57cm
5¾"	14.5cm	23"	58.5cm
6"	15cm	24"	61cm
6¼"	16cm	26"	66cm
6½"	16.5cm	27"	68.5cm
7"	18cm	28"	71cm
7½"	19cm	32"	81cm
7¾"	19.5cm	4yd	3.5m
8"	20.5cm	5yd	4.5m
9"	23cm	12yd	11m
10"	25.5cm	20yd	18m
11¾"	30cm	100yd	91.5m
12"	30.5cm	184yd	168m
12½"	32cm	220yd	201m
13"	33cm	437yd	399.5m

OUR MISSION

A portion of the author's proceeds from this book will be donated to a fertility chapter to assist couples in need of financial aid in order to grow their families. Our mission is to aid couples who cannot afford fertility treatments, such as in vitro fertilization (IVF), that are not covered by health insurance, and also to assist with adoption.